THE
BEDSIT
SURVIVAL
MANUAL

THE
BEDSIT
SURVIVAL
MANUAL

DAVID HALLAMSHIRE

EBURY PRESS & LONDON

To my parents for being great people and to
anyone who blows up the bedsit with the red and
white striped wallpaper in Leeds.

Published by Ebury Press
Division of The National Magazine Company Ltd
Colquhoun House
27-37 Broadwick Street
London W1V 1FR

First impression 1988
Text copyright © 1988 David Hallamshire
Illustrations copyright © 1988 Nigel Paige

ISBN 0 85223 760 X

Edited by Miren Lopategui
Designed by Jerry Goldie

Typeset by Textype Typesetters, Cambridge
Printed and bound in Great Britain by
Butler & Tanner Limited, Frome and London

CONTENTS

HOW TO USE THIS BOOK

Start at the beginning
and read all the words
one after the other until
you come to the very
end and then stop.

CHAPTER ONE

THE ROOM

The first experience anyone has of living in a bedsit is when they occupy their mother's womb. This is dark and lonely and surrounded by funny noises too. However, when you *do* move into a proper bedsit you will notice the difference immediately. The ceiling is a lot higher.

The classic bedsit ceiling is so high that the air changes pressure between the floor and the curtain rail. This feature is incorporated to enable you to be miserably cold in winter and yet miserably cold in summer.

If you move into a bedsit which is described as furnished, you will notice this as soon as you walk into the room. Scattered around the vast expanse of worn-out carpet will be various objects that on closer inspection can be identified as furniture. These usually consist of a chair, a bed, a table and maybe a wardrobe or chest of drawers. (The black thing in the corner is the cooker.)

Your first reaction when entering a bedsit will be to open the curtains and let more light in. It will be then that you notice that the curtains are in fact open and you are facing on to the back alley of an Indian restaurant. Endless hours of fun can be spent watching the population of alley cats increasing and decreasing each week.

Incidentally, the holes in the wallpaper are caused by hundreds of people having stuck little blue balls of sticky stuff like plasticine to the walls when putting up posters. The way to remove this is to pull it off the wall very quickly so that the wallpaper rips, leaving a neat jagged hole.

It is always worth looking through the drawers of the furniture that best resembles a chest of drawers, if only to prove that everyone that ever lived in a bedsit leaves a pin in the top drawer and had a leaky Biro.

One of the items that is a world standard is a globe lampshade, made from paper, that folds flat when rested on the floor. This can be found in nearly every bedsit in the world. The person who has escaped from bedsit land will experience recurring panic attacks should he ever walk into a room and see a lampshade of this type. The very presence of it will bring back memories of sleepless nights spent on a lumpy mattress listening to rock music coming through the floor. The smell of cabbage will also drift into mind.

Therefore, one of the first things to do when moving into a bedsit is to buy a new lampshade. If you do this you can say you are living in a flat.

Probably the most fascinating thing that you will notice about your new bedsit is the colour of the paint used on the door and the window frame. This is a particular type of paint known as Bedsit White and has astounding properties.

When the paint is applied it is a bright white colour. On exposure to the air, however, it will change slowly to a depressing mustard brown. It should be noted that this change is temperature-sensitive and from the floor to the ceiling the colour graduates from a pale milky yellow to a deep rich nicotine brown.

This paint goes on in six coats at once and assumes different colours at the different layers. Proof of this can be seen around the door frame and windowsill where the paint has been chipped. The most common colour for the third and fifth layers is chocolate brown or dark blue.

Bedsit White will also crack around the door frame and window frame within minutes of application. This is to allow draughts to come soaring through the gaps in winter.

Having had a good look at your new surroundings you should now begin to put posters up. Posters are put up to cover over all the little holes in the wall where people once put posters up. The best type of posters should show in no uncertain terms your political, musical, artistic and sexual preferences. These should be put up as soon as possible to give you a sense of belonging and to establish your territory. Cats and dogs do this by urinating in the corners of their territory. This is only because they don't have any posters. (*Note:* Some people prefer to put up framed pictures. These people are not true bedsit-landers and would be better suited to living in a flat with boring neighbours and a rubber plant called Fred.)

The next thing to do when moving into your new bedsit is to set up your stereo and play your favourite record at full volume while you are unpacking hundreds of cardboard boxes. This helps make the task a little more enjoyable and also lets the neighbours know you have arrived. It is also a primitive way of claiming your

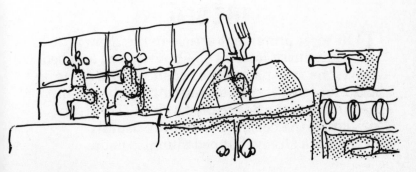

11

territory. Birds do this by singing songs that are unique to their species. This is only because they don't have stereos.

· ·

If you don't have any posters and you don't have a stereo you could always urinate in the corner of the room.

· ·

Having put up your posters and blown the dust out of your speakers you should then go about the task of making the bed. It is strongly advised that you put a blanket over the mattress as quickly as possible and then put a sheet on top of that. This will save you from being horribly disturbed by the 'coffee' stains on the mattress.

THE BED

T he most prominent article in the room is a flat dusty-looking object described as a bed. This is the 'bed' part of the bedsit. This is not to be confused with the bulging collapsed mess in the middle of the floor called a chair. This is the 'sit' part of the bedsit. The posture usually adopted is a slump, but bed-slump is not a

12

commercially viable description when renting out a room.

Bedsit mattresses come in various forms but the most common types are the Flop Drop mattress and the Rock mattress.

THE FLOP DROP MATTRESS

This is a standard mattress that has been cultivated over many years and by many people so that there is an absence of stuffing in the middle of the mattress. If a tentative inspection is made by pressing on the mattress with your foot, a high-quality Flop Drop mattress will enable you to feel the bed springs through it.

Strangely enough, the Flop Drop mattress usually sits on a base with a concave curve because all the springs collapsed years ago.

These mattresses are especially good for back ache. Nothing will give you back ache quicker than a Flop Drop mattress.

THE ROCK MATTRESS

The alternative to the Flop Drop mattress is a cunningly designed mattress immediately recognized by its convex curve. This mattress has no spring in it whatsoever and will encourage you to roll out of bed at every opportunity. This is especially effective when used with a duvet.

The Rock mattress also tends to sit on a bed base that is on the verge of collapse and has been covered with a piece of hardboard.

13

. . . .

At no time should you ever leap on to a bedsit mattress. The resultant injuries are just not worth it and the dust will take weeks to clear.

. . . .

Rock mattresses are particularly useful if you happen to be a gangster as they will stop bullets at point blank range.

Having made the bed, it is now time to look around the room and study the other items of 'furniture'.

THE CHAIR

I n the middle of the floor will be the 'chair'. Given time you will come to despise and loathe the chair almost as much as the bed. What the bed hasn't done in crippling a perfectly good spine the chair will do without any trouble.

The most noticeable thing about a bedsit chair is the way it makes you sit like a gorilla, with your knuckles on the floor, your shoulders arched and your knees up round your neck somewhere.

14

The bedsit chair comes in many styles, the only common feature being that it is as comfortable to sit on as a bag of marbles. The deluxe model incorporates a bump under one buttock, a slight lean to one side and a wobble.

Invest in a bean bag immediately on moving into a bedsit and whenever a guest comes round offer them the chair. They will think you are doing them a favour until they sit on it.

(It is always worth bearing in mind that you can set fire to the chair in winter.)

THE WARDROBE

The wardrobe is a large box made during the war that leans at a funny angle to the wall. This is for putting metal coat hangers in.

In a top-quality bedsit wardrobe the door always falls open no matter how carefully you try and get the catch to hold it shut. A way of overcoming this problem is to lean things up against the door. Another way is to rip the door off and pretend it is a Swedish open plan wardrobe.

The most popular use of the wardrobe is for putting cardboard boxes and suitcases on top of. No bedsit wardrobe would be complete without a smart collection of empty supermarket boxes littering the top of it. You may even find that these boxes become like old friends and for no reason such phrases as '12 doz packs' and 'Weetabix' float through your subconscious.

Never trust anyone that hasn't got a suitcase

on their wardrobe. This means they are travelling light and are just using the room for sex and illegal pastimes. Either that or they are spies.

THE TABLE

Not all bedsits have a table. This is no great loss as the table is useless anyway, because a succession of people have stood on it, sat on it and rested their feet on it. This abuse gives the table a dramatic wobble. The wobble is so great that the only people that can eat off the table are bus conductors and British Rail waiters.

The bedsit table also has a collection of burn marks and coffee stains that no amount of cleaning will remove. The burn marks are quite interesting because when you become really bored you can put your fingernail under the flaking varnish and flick little bits off on to the carpet. You will notice your friends doing this whenever they come round.

At no time should you stand on a bedsit table. All bedsit tables have one leg that has been glued back in place, so that the landlord doesn't know someone has wrecked it. What most people don't know is that the table was a write-off anyway and it was the landlord that glued the leg on in the first place.

· ·

Tables burn really well in winter.

16

CHAPTER TWO

THE SHARED KITCHEN

Some bedsits do in fact have a large separate kitchen used by several occupants of the house. This does sometimes cause problems to develop, and can cause minor rifts in the friendly community.

One of the most common problems that a newcomer faces is finding somewhere to put up notices telling people to keep off his things. This problem arises because the walls are already covered with them. For some strange reason the cupboard with the biggest Keep Out notice only contains a tin of peaches and a tin of processed peas with a rusty lid.

The newcomer to a shared kitchen should note that he is not to be distressed by the smell of cabbage. This smell is very common, in spite of the fact that not one single person is ever seen cooking it.

Also note that the black carbon coated hole underneath the rings of the cooker is called the 'oven'. This large storage space is for hiding bottles of cider in during parties. No other application has ever been seen.

The best way of dealing with someone that keeps using your milk is to take them quietly to one side and kick them in the throat.

THE PEDAL BIN

The pedal bin is always full. Even when you have only just emptied it. If the pedal bin is in a shared kitchen it will always be you that empties it, no matter how long you try to ignore it. Everyone else will claim that they are the only person that ever empties it, but this simply isn't true.

After several years of living in a bedsit or shared house you will make an amazing discovery. The pedal bin is where the smell of cabbage comes from. There will never be any cabbage in it, but that's where the smell comes from. Sometimes this smell can be masked with the odour of old cheese and putrid milk.

One of the things you will notice about the pedal bin is that it doesn't have a pedal. The ones that actually do have a pedal only open the lid just high enough for you to have to bend down and lift the lid properly. This is quite common. If you buy a pedal bin that does open the lid properly when you press the pedal, you have bought a fake. Some really bad fakes don't even smell of cabbage.

· ·

Getting a bigger bin makes no difference. It will still always be you that has to empty it.

· ·

Many ingenious methods are used to make the pedal bin even more full than it already is so that you don't have to go and empty it. One usually involves a delicate building up of cans and milk cartons so that it looks like a sculpture of domestic rubbish in mid explosion. This build-up usually ceases when as many cans and cartons fall off the bin as you are trying to put on at the same time.

THE WASHING MACHINE

T he role of the communal washing machine is to go 'Chuggedy chuggedy' and throw water all over the floor. They are only found in shared kitchens and tend to be used either every three weeks or whenever everyone in the house is trying to cook a meal at the same time.

The only real pleasure to be gained from a washing machine is when you are watching someone else trying to use it. Especially when they come to the 'I wonder what this does?' part. This usually means that a lot of water is going to come out of it any second.

The other good bit is when the clothes are being spun dry. Not only does this cause a lot of water to go all over the floor but it usually results in the machine suddenly lurching across the floor until the victim is pinned against the sink. This would be funny in itself, but the humour is enhanced by the fact that it looks like the twin tub is engaged in some sort of erotic activity with the victim.

The only people that have any great success in using the communal washing machine are nurses. They do this by either bossing it into submission, or putting a half Nelson on it and forcing it to work. Naturally, this is only done for the washing machine's own good.

Bank clerks under eight stone and people that press wild flowers should avoid going near the communal washing machine. Washing machines know a safe bet when they see one and will have your arm off at the elbow before you know it.

Washing machines really do have a life of their own and you should be careful not to put anything valuable in the spin dryer, like your head or your hand.

THE WATER GEYSER

T his is not the man from the Water Board. This is a plastic container that has a heating element in it and is located on the wall above the sink. The geyser is used to save money on hot water. It does this by taking so long to boil that you give up and think of something else to do.

It is always worth checking just how powerful the flow of water from the tap is, before fitting the geyser's plastic tube to it. The way this is supposed to work is that the tube fits over the tap like a hose-pipe and when the tap is turned on the geyser fills with water. What usually happens is that there is a loud 'Gerdoosh!' and you get soaked when the tube blows off the tap.

21

The water geyser also has the habit of making a tremendous noise just when the most important line of dialogue is being spoken on the film you are watching. As well as being annoying it can be quite a shock, as it will have been several hours since you turned it on.

When this happens, be sure to look absently round the room trying to remember what you were boiling water for.

THE FRIDGE

I f you are living in a one-room bedsit and you have a fridge, you should immediately put a curtain across the middle of the room and call it a Flatlette. This is because the fridge is normally only found in shared kitchens. The reason for this is that if it is in the same room that you are sleeping in, it drives you mad every time it goes 'Kerticker ticker ticker hummmmm' every hour or so. Also, when it stops you tend to wind up the nearest clock.

The shared fridge is divided into several compartments where each person in the house keeps their own personal food. These unmarked divisions should not be crossed. People tend to be very possessive about their piece of shelf and any attempt to hustle your sausages alongside their yogurt will result in remarks like 'What's *that* doing there!' The offending article will then be moved to another part of the fridge.

If you are a newcomer and nobody has told you where your part of the fridge is, simply leave a package of Danish Blue on the most full shelf and see where it comes to rest after several days. It can then be assumed that this is your part of the fridge.

There is a process associated with the fridge called 'defrosting'. This should be done when you can no longer get things into the freezer compartment because of ice taking up all the room.

Defrosting involves piling everyone's food on the kitchen table while the fridge drips water all over the floor. If there is a drip tray, do not be alarmed when a flood of water goes down one arm and on to the floor when you try and empty it in the sink. This is quite common and is all part of the fun of defrosting, as is the irresistible urge to poke the soggy packet of peas with your finger.

Games to play with fridges

1. Count how many people say 'Oh. Is it defrosting?' when you defrost the fridge.

2. Climb inside the fridge and see if the light goes off when the door shuts.

3. Try and get out of the fridge without calling for help.

4. Leave somebody's underwear in the icebox for two hours and then put it back on the washing line.

CHAPTER THREE

THE BEDSIT BATHROOM

When you first move into a bedsit one of the strange rituals that you will need to observe is cleaning the bath. In bedsit land you will need to clean the bath 'before' you get into it rather than when you get out of it. It also helps the water drain if you remove the horrible gunk of matted hair from the plughole. This should be done every year or so.

One of the delightful aspects of bedsit baths is that they tend to be genuine relics from the Romans. They are of such a size that you can actually learn to swim in them. Non-swimmers are advised to stay away from the tap end of the bath. Water skiing is not recommended as the overflowing water will fuse the lights of the person living downstairs and could upset them.

A further point to remember before taking a bath is to remove the spider. This spider is a standard feature of the bedsit called a Boris Bathus. This hardy breed of spider has evolved over many years and specializes in climbing halfway up the side of the bath and then turning round and sliding all the way down again. They must enjoy it, because that's all they ever seem to do. It is pointless trying to flush this creature down the plug hole as it will only climb back up and push out the plug when you least expect it.

A much better way of removing the spider is to side swipe it with a towel or actually remove it with your hands. A lot of people find that the latter action is best if accompanied by the word 'Eeaargh!'.

At no time while taking a bath will you ever see the Toilet Roll Fairy. This is a strange phenomenon common to bedsit land and shared houses. The following things are known about the Toilet Roll Fairy:

1. It is the Toilet Roll Fairy that will make any toilet roll disappear if it is left unattended in the bathroom for more than five minutes. All enquiries as to its whereabouts will produce a collection of blank expressions.

2. The Toilet Roll Fairy puts up abusive notices in the bathroom telling people to clean the bath after use. It is only the Toilet Roll Fairy that could have done this, because everyone will deny all knowledge of them, with such phrases as 'Yerwhat?' and 'It weren't me pal.'

3. The Toilet Roll Fairy is the person that took all the hot water when you were wanting a bath.

4. The Toilet Roll Fairy is the presence in the bathroom every single morning without fail when you are busting for a pee, and yet is never seen leaving.

Nobody knows why the person who had 16 curries and a gallon of real ale the night before always uses the bathroom just before you have a bath.

The distribution of bath times is a delicate thing and should be adhered to rigidly. Failure to do so can lead to people kicking the door down in frustration because you are in the bath when they think they should be. This leads to them being in the bath when someone else usually is, until it gets to the point where people barricade themselves in the bathroom all day to ensure they get a bath when they want one.

A way of overcoming this is to have a bath at three o'clock in the morning. Though this isn't foolproof. Especially if someone is having a party. The locks on the bathroom door aren't always very good and it can lead to embarrassment having several people stagger in and out when you are playing with your duck.

27

Interesting things to do in the bath

1. Find the plug for the plug hole.

2. See how big you can make a wave without it flopping out of the bath on to your clothes.

3. When someone comes to the door to see if anyone is in the bath, say things like, 'Lower. Just there. Oooh.'

4. Make goals out of your feet and fire soap out of your hands at them.

5. Listen to the radio underwater.

6. Pretend you are Tarzan and wrestle with the bath duck.

7. Swim one length underwater.

8. Paint yourself black and pretend you are a killer whale or a submarine, depending on your mood.

9. Pretend you are a blue whale and save yourself from extinction.

10. Stand up and look at your feet to see what you look like with short legs.

CHAPTER FOUR

COOKING IN A BEDSIT

A s previously mentioned, the black charred-looking thing is the cooker. This can take on various forms but, ideally, to reach a peak of frustration and depression common to bedsit land, it should be a two-ring burner with a wobble.

If a four-ring cooker with oven is provided, its ideal location is right against the corner of the room. This causes a fascinating clash of pan handles over the middle of the cooker and virtually renders the wallside rings useless.

In the more upmarket bedsits the room has what is called a kitchenette. This is a cupboard with a cooker in it. Rent is usually increased because of the existence of this high-class facility. Really classy kitchenettes have a multi-coloured plastic thing that dangles in front of the door and collects grease. Hairdressers and tacky trinket shops also use multi-coloured plastic dangly things over the door. The people who own these shops are usually landlords.

(One of the more interesting points of a bedsit cooker is that no matter how many times the grill pan is cleaned there will always be remnants of cheese on toast in it when you come to use it.)

The best time to cook in a bedsit is never. However, if you really must cook, open all the windows so that the mysterious smell of cabbage can get out and the smell of Indian or Chinese cooking can get in from the Take Away across the road.

The easiest way of cooking anything on a bedsit cooker is to either fry it or put it in a big pot and stir it round and round, adding Oxo cubes as you go until it no longer tastes like beans on toast or cabbage.

If you ever do cook cabbage, which nobody in their right mind would, simply allow it to boil furiously with the lid off the pan until it becomes a sloshy green mulch then throw it away.

On rainy days, when things are becoming very boring and there aren't any vegetarians to taunt, go to your local library and steal all the books about 'Cooking For One'. These are very funny and will help you to while away the afternoon. The really good bit is the one about the half-aubergine and the left-over pepper and the cup of prawns.

Following the instructions is easy if you just happen to have the left-overs from a banquet for 20. The bit that will make you cry with laughter is when you are told to add two spoonfuls of 'fresh cream' to pea soup and put it in 'your blender' for 30 seconds. (A blender, by the way, is a thing that you put food in and it all goes round and round until it looks like sick.)

The only book written about cooking for one that makes any sense is called *Cooking in a*

30

Bedsitter by Katharine Whitehorn. This book hardly ever mentions cabbage. It is also exactly one centimetre thick and can be used for measuring things.

All the other books about cooking for one are written by people that have never lived on their own in their lives and have four kids to eat all the bits of things left over from their stupid recipes. Where does 'half a pepper' come from? Where did the other half go? Where can you buy two tablespoons of cream from? When did you ever see anyone in a bedsit with a blender? What idiot actually eats cabbage anyway? These questions are never answered.

Never wipe anything off the cooker as it will soon turn to a very hard black material which will protect the white enamel surface from scratching. Should you decide at any time to try and remove the black coating, the best advice is, don't. Diamond grinding wheels are very expensive and if you do ever get the cooker looking white you will be forever wiping things off it when you should be concentrating on more important things, like where the funny smell is coming from and whether you've got enough Oxo cubes to make cheese on toast.

Typical 'Cooking For One' Recipe
Pig's trotter soup

1. Take one pig's trotter from a left-over pig. (The rest of the pig can be used later.)

2. Add half an aubergine and half a red pepper.

3. Mix thoroughly in your blender for 13.2 seconds.

4. Sauté half a cow and add 2 ounces to the mixture.

5. Add 2 tablespoons of fresh cream and sprinkle with parsley.

6. Serve with red wine, beef, Yorkshire pudding, roast potatoes and gravy.

A Real 'Cooking For One' Recipe

1. Take 2 cans of stuff with different-coloured labels.

2. Pour both into a big pot.

3. Heat up and add Oxo until brown.

4. Eat.

Interesting things to do with eggs

1. Stand one egg on end for 5 minutes.

2. Boil 6 eggs for exactly 3 minutes and see if any of them don't still look disgusting when you take the top off.

3. Put 2 egg whites in a hanky and go round pretending you have just blown your nose.

4. See how many eggs you can get in your underpants without breaking more than two.

5. See how tough an egg is by placing your palms flat against each end and pressing hard enough to make it explode all over the kitchen.

6. Place a raw egg in a cup. Add milk and pepper and drink in one go without being sick.

How to cook cabbage

1. # Don't.

CHAPTER FIVE

NEIGHBOURS

Although the bedsit is a self-contained unit, there can be four or five of them in one house. These are also occupied by bedsit-landers. You should note that no matter how many different places you eventually live in and no matter how many people you come across, it will always be you that is the most sociable, quiet, likeable, sober and hygenic.

In fact, compared with the drug addicts and pimps and sex maniacs and lunatics and weirdos that can be found in bedsits, you will regard yourself as some sort of superior being. There is absolutely nothing wrong with this attitude even if you do take drugs, drink, smell and talk to yourself. What do they know anyway?

THE HEAVY METAL HERO

Many different types of people are found in bedsits, but probably the hardest to live with (or above) is the Heavy Metal Hero. The Heavy Metal Hero, as the name suggests, listens to loud rock music at uncomfortable volumes. That is, uncomfortable for you, not them. Heavy Metal Heroes have no feeling in their heads, as is constantly demonstrated when they insist on hitting hard surfaces with them. Under some circumstances their music would be quite acceptable had you not heard all their records ten years ago.

One of the interesting features of Heavy Metal Heroes is that they rarely play music during the day. They save this pleasure until after 1.30 a.m. If the Heavy Metal Hero is heard playing music in the afternoon or normal hours of the day it would be a neighbourly act to go round and see if he is all right.

A good way of combating the effects of music played in the early hours of the morning is to find out where the fuse-box is. It is then a simple matter to remove his fuse and go back to bed. Great pleasure can be had from those first few seconds of silence when he thinks he has gone deaf and blind.

A lot of fun can also be had from putting the fuse back in the fuse-box at 9.30 in the morning and listening to the sudden impact of Whitesnake blowing his speakers out.

THE PUNK

In spite of the reputation the Punk may have, he is easier to live with than the Heavy Metal Hero. This is due to the fact that the Punk tends to play his music from 5 p.m. until 11 p.m. continuously.

This terrorizing of the eardrums can be avoided if you go to the pub at 5 p.m. and come back at 11 p.m. Many students adopt this timetable for drinking. This is not to avoid punk music though. This is because they are all drunken degenerates anyway.

Punks are especially handy to know if you need a safety pin.

THE STUDENT

Students come in many forms and cross all barriers including the Heavy Metal Hero and the Punk. Nearly all of them are called Derek or Adrian and come from Newcastle or a snotty suburb on the outskirts of London. Those that don't, come from Bristol.

First-year Students are the hardest to live with as they have just discovered sex and alcohol and talk about them all the time. The best Students to live with are dead ones, but if that is not possible the next best thing is an alcoholic tramp as they don't talk about sex all the time and have the decency to fall down when they get drunk.

The most difficult time to live in a bedsit with a Student as a neighbour is around exam time. It is interesting to observe that at this time they go particularly moody and hang infantile signs on their doors like 'Keep Out' and 'Piss Off'. It is usually in your interests to observe their request for quiet as you should take advantage of the silence while it lasts.

After the exams it is a different story, as the Student frequently indulges in all-night drinking and late-night sex. At this stage of course it is worth befriending the Student and helping him to finish off his drink and his girlfriend.

If you find that a neighbour is a Student and also a member of the Rugby Club, it is best to move out. A normal human being can only stand so many renditions of 'The Good Ship Venus' and 'Swing Low Sweet Chariot'.

THE CND VEGETARIAN

Not all vegetarians support CND. Not all CND members are vegetarian. But it helps. The CND Vegetarian feels a great need to communicate with people by sticking posters on the outside of his door. The content of which is usually to do with bombs or monkeys with wires coming out of their heads.

The CND Vegetarian comes in two types. One is very thin and pale and would have liked to have been a hippy but wasn't born early enough. The other is thin and pale and *was* a hippy. Both types like talking about the threat of nuclear war and animals that you only ever see on posters.

. . . .

Hippies were people who used to spend all day having sex and finding interesting ways to destroy their brain cells.

37

These people are very difficult to live with in a shared house as their main hobby is sitting in the communal kitchen and acting disgusted when you are trying to cook a perfectly good steak. The only way to get back at them is to get in the kitchen early in the morning and fill the place with the smell of bacon. This is guaranteed to put them off their raisins and sawdust.

Another good way of getting back at the CND Vegetarian who has totally destroyed your enjoyment of beef casserole is to leave a half-mutilated chicken in the fridge. This upsets them a great deal and is a real laugh.

At no time should you ever attempt to discuss Nuclear War with such people. It is their life's obsession and they will have read a lot more leaflets about it than you have. They also have the inability to explain things in simple terms. They will tell you with great enthusiasm the economic, political, emotional and physical effect of a single bomb falling on a city the size of Sheffield and did you see *Threads* wasn't it awful etc. Where as what they really mean is that if a bomb drops on you it will make you dead.

THE NUISANCE

T he Nuisance has no outstanding qualities other than being a pain in the neck. The most common activity of these people is knocking on people's doors very lightly and then standing back and smiling broadly as they ask you: (a) Do you know where the vacuum cleaner is? (b) Can you 'lend' 50 pence? (c) Do you know anything about televisions?

All these questions would be quite inoffensive if it were not for their being asked three times a day.

The Nuisance has the uncanny ability to disturb you at exactly the moment when you don't want to be disturbed. This is usually three minutes into your favourite programme, during your favourite passage of music, when you have just come back from the pub, or, more especially, when you are reclining on top of your loved one, whispering sweet nothings like 'Faster' and 'Uph--Uph--Uph'.

The Nuisance has a very low IQ and will be totally oblivious to you shouting 'What now!' loud enough for them to hear it through the door just before you open it. In fact the only response you can get from a Nuisance is to tell him to 'Bugger off' and shut the door. This won't actually make such people go away but will give you 30 seconds peace while they stand there confused, wondering what you meant. This is usually followed by a light knock on the door.

THE LUNATIC

No matter where you live in bedsitland you will eventually encounter the Lunatic. The most interesting ones are the types with aggressive tendencies, providing of course that it isn't you that is tending to get in the way of their aggression.

The Lunatic is usually in his mid-thirties and without exception is male. Very few women in their thirties live in bedsits. Especially Lunatic ones. All the Lunatic women have become Councillors or Social Workers by the time they reach their thirties.

It is uncertain why Lunatics are in their mid-thirties but anyone aspiring to be an aggressive schizophrenic should attempt to make their neurosis peak at that age in order to fit into the jovial hurly-burly of bedsitland. An attempt should also be made to gather a large collection of milk bottle tops or bus timetables in order to capture people on the landing and discusss them in great depth.

The Lunatic makes no sense when he talks to you and wears clothes that are exactly 13 years out of date. Usually, garments such as nylon anoraks, orange corduroy trousers with bell bottoms and bri-nylon shirts are the key components of his wardrobe. Added glamour is achieved if he wears black glasses with discoloured sellotape holding the frame together at one side.

Approaches to the Lunatic during the day

should be avoided at all costs. At night as well, come to think of it. This is because no sensible conversation is possible. The Lunatic will only tell you of his anxiety about something that makes you go 'Eh?' and wish you had pretended you hadn't seen him, like you usually do.

The Lunatic is the person that you can hear having an animated conversation with himself at three o'clock in the morning. This is usually followed by such activities as slamming the doors and vacuuming the ceiling.

THE LEFT-WING ULTRA-FEMINIST

The actual room of a Left-Wing Ultra-Feminist can be identified without actually seeing its occupant. All you have to do is count the words on the many posters and leaflets displayed prominently on the outside of the door and see how many times the word 'Women' appears.

If the word 'Wimmin' appears, it is better in the long run to move out as you will be pinned up against the wall at every opportunity and told, if male, how ignorant you are, and, if female, how suppressed you are. The best reply at all times is 'Yes'.

Luckily the Left-Wing Ultra-Feminist is not that difficult to live with as she refuses to cook because it is demeaning, won't talk to males (demeaning), won't associate with married women (all suppressed) and spends most of her time at rallies in support of a little-known political cause in a hot country somewhere. The

Left-Wing Ultra-Feminist sometimes leaves a packet of big cotton earplugs on the bathroom shelf that allow you to ski, swim and dance with confidence.

THE PHANTOM NEIGHBOUR

You will know exactly when the Phantom Neighbour goes to work because you can hear him every morning, getting up, putting the radio on, padding around and going out of the front door. You will also know exactly when he comes back from work because the door can be heard opening and closing every evening.

You will know what sort of music he likes because you can hear it through the door as you pass by and you may even know what food he likes from the smells drifting along the corridor. Yet you will never see him. Ever.

It can go on for months. You can even try rushing out into the hallway as you hear the door opening and he will dip back into his room for something. Or you can chase him as you hear the front door closing and all you will see is a leg disappearing around the corner. The reason for this is that the Phantom Neighbour is in fact a Spy. This is obvious, because when you knock on his door to borrow something he will pretend to be out. Even when he *is* out. Only Spies can do this.

CHAPTER SIX

BEDSIT AILMENTS

J ust as playing tennis can give you tennis elbow and playing the violin at night can result in severe blows to the head, there are common ailments associated with living in a bedsit.

BEDSIT SHIN

T his is a red itchy scale which develops on the shin bone. It usually occurs in winter and is caused by having to sit so close to the fire that – although the rest of your body is freezing – your trouser legs are scorching. The smell of very hot material can be ignored provided it does not take on the smell of bacon.

A way of overcoming Bedsit Shin is to wear football pads. A better way of overcoming the problem is to wear the patented Bedsit Survival Suit (see p. 52).

BEDSIT HAND

P eople suffering from Bedsit Hand are easily identifiable by the fact that they become nervous and jittery when required to light the gas fire. The physical effects of Bedsit Hand are a scorching of the back of the hand and a noticeable patch of singed hair on the right forearm.

This is caused by the gas fire's own battery ignition system having long since failed and requiring to be lit by matches. The result of lighting a bedsit gas fire with matches is that for several seconds nothing happens at all. This momentary silence is followed by a loud explosion which blows the bedsitlander backwards and singes his hand in the process.

The condition is overcome by hiding behind the chair and throwing lit matches at the gas fire. This should be done very quickly after turning the gas on as it can lead to embarrassment when your windows blow out.

BEDSIT NOSE

B edsit Nose is a condition which makes the sufferer look alcoholic. The nose assumes a bright red blotchy complexion in contrast to the rest of the face, which is usually pale white with grey sunken eye sockets.

Bedsit Nose occurs in winter and is due to the fact that the nose is the only part of the body that protrudes from the duvet into the sub-zero temperatures in the room.

The fact that you are suffering from Bedsit Nose can be disguised by becoming alcoholic.

HEATING IN A BEDSIT

Heating is the biggest problem that anyone encounters when they move into a bedsit. One of the main reasons for this is the high ceiling which was built in the days when people used to burn servants to keep warm.

It is always worth while having an abundant supply of 50-pence pieces and an industrial funnel. This will enable you to pour enough money into the meter so that you can sit down for a few seconds in front of the fire before it goes off again. In summer it should be noted that it is possible (after using a hammer and chisel on the window frame) to open the window and let some warm air in.

Friends calling unexpectedly can cause a great deal of embarrassment in winter as they tend to live in warm centrally heated houses (the swines!) and are not aware of the problem. They will find it hysterical to catch you wearing orange ski socks and woolly hat with ear-flaps. Simply say 'Yes' when they say 'Cor, it's cold in here intit?'. Physical violence will only warm you up for a short time and isn't worth the effort.

A handy hint for the DIY enthusiast is to

46

double glaze the windows with miles of sticky tape and hundreds of plastic bags. Large clear plastic bags are the best as things like 'Sunblest' and 'Top Shop' don't let very much light in and start getting on your nerves around April.

A cheap way of heating the room in winter is to invite as many friends back to the bedsit as possible and ask them all to breathe heavily. Through the walls this will sound like a mass orgy and bring even more people into the room, thereby cutting your bills further.

It is a good idea to keep a box of matches nearby. They will be useful when the lights suddenly go out and when you get really depressed in January you can strike one and see what warmth looks like.

. . . .

Although duffel coats, woolly hats and Balaclavas are recommended on very cold nights it is inadvisable to wear ski boots as they catch on the duvet.

47

If there are any old aged pensioners nearby, ask them to keep popping in to see if you are all right. It will keep you active by having to answer the door and may save you from dying. The most dangerous thing about hypothermia is that nobody tells you you are dead.

Should you find yourself shivering violently and pacing up and down slapping your hands together, do not be alarmed. This is an indication that you are not dead. Keep this up until you either feel better or go round to the old aged pensioners' to get warm.

. . . .

TV sets don't burn very well.

If things get really bad you can erect a tent in the middle of the floor and try keeping that warm instead of the whole room. This will give you the added status of having an extra room and you can say you are living in a flat. Don't leave it up when the landlord comes round, however, as he will only put your rent up. If you still find you can't afford the heating you can always put another tent up and get a lodger.

If you get really depressed go round and see another bedsitlander. It will be a great boost to your morale to see someone else wearing six duffel coats and living in a tent in the middle of the room.

· ·

Tents don't burn for very long.

49

Get a fat lover in October. They tend to get snapped up by November.

Getting out of bed can be difficult at the best of times but in winter in a bedsit it is nearly impossible. The temperature at three o'clock in the morning can be as low as 2 degrees Kelvin. (Kelvin was a man who lived in a bedsit. The coldest it got was zero degrees Kelvin.)

The most difficult personal conflict you will ever have in your life is when you wake up at three o'clock in the morning and have a bladder that sounds like a ripe melon when you tap it. This urgent need to relieve your bladder is in direct conflict with the need to avoid frostbite, should you actually venture out of bed.

The agony of this situation is enhanced by the fact that the toilet is two flights of stairs and a corridor away. This will lead you to moan sleepily and try to find a position where your bladder doesn't hurt as much. However, the relief is short-lived and you will eventually have to face the fact that you will be required to put on your Antarctic gear and go to the toilet.

A strange mental process also takes place around this time. Although the very last thing you wanted last Christmas was a pair of slippers and a big fluffy tartan dressing gown, you will begin to curse your friends and relatives for not buying you a pair of slippers and a big fluffy tartan dressing gown. 'All I wanted was a big fluffy tartan dressing gown.' This will all be forgotten in the morning.

Most people that get out of bed will then use the sink for their light relief. Nobody will actually admit to doing this but 2 degrees Kelvin is no joke and you will do anything, but

. . . .

Physical jerks are not recommended as the house will be full of them already.

. . . .

Exercises for keeping warm

1. Put on three pullovers.

2. Slap your hands together.

3. Go to the pub.

4. Come back from the pub.

5. Put on another three pullovers.

6. Go to bed with a good book and somebody else.

51

anything, just to be able to go back to bed and avoid having to go down two flights of stairs and a corridor.

When you go back to bed you will curl up in a little ball in the middle of the bed and let out a pained groan. You should then drift back to sleep, dreaming of big fluffy tartan dressing gowns.

THE PATENTED BEDSIT SURVIVAL SUIT

One of the more dignified ways of dressing to overcome the cold is to wear the Patented Bedsit Survival Suit. This is an ingenious, one-piece, duckdown-lined jump-suit with pockets for added accessories including a soundproof hood and a blackout visor for when you wish to go to sleep.

The pockets can also hold a good book and sandwiches to while away those lonely hours. A special battery is fitted for the internal heating coils and protective materials are used, as in heatproof shin pads and flameproof mittens to prevent such common ailments as Bedsit Shin and Bedsit Hand.

A handy hint for those who have managed to fill the meter with enough money to keep the fire going is to place a cardboard box or shield in front of the meter. This prevents the draught from the fly wheel blowing the fire out. (This does not apply to people with electric fires. You'd never be able to earn that much money.)

CHAPTER EIGHT

HOW TO BE DRUNK IN A BEDSIT

The best advice to anyone coming back to a bedsit drunk, is to immediately shut the door and fall down. It is difficult enough moving round a bedsit when sober but the simple yet effective touch of falling down can prevent serious injury.

It is especially important that nothing you see should be eaten whilst lying on the floor, no matter how interesting it may look. Many wood lice have met their deaths by being mistaken for peanuts.

If you are capable of lifting your nose off the floor you will be able to see under the bed. This is quite a frightening experience and should not be indulged in too often as you will not be able to sleep knowing that you are just inches from a jungle of crumbs, dust and pubic hair.

Should you have overcome the trauma of seeing under the bed the next move is to try and get into it. A useful technique is to crawl on all fours. Be sure to lift your head off the carpet as failure to do so can result in a form of Bedsit Nose.

After reaching the bed the most popular position to adopt is Position 6. This is where your knees are actually on the floor while the top half of your body is slumped on the bed with arms splayed out. The head should be rested at a sharp 90 degree angle to prevent you suffocating on your duvet. The accomplishment of this position is usually accompanied by the word 'Ohphookimle'.

Some bedsitlanders choose to occupy this position for several hours at a time, depending on their state of intoxication. The main disadvantage of assuming this position for long periods of time is that when you do wake up you will think you have broken your neck.

The less hardy amongst you will find that Position 6 can only be achieved for a short time before there is a violent need to be sick.

On no account stand up!

Standing up usually results in severe injury. Those people who do venture into the upright position will notice a dramatic lack of blood to the head and will begin to move sideways at a high speed.

The tendency is to try and counteract this movement by sticking one leg in the air. However, you will then become aware that it is needed on the floor in the direction of travel. Further movements like this take place but your body will seem determined to venture the length of the room at high velocity.

With luck you will be stopped by the back of the armchair hitting you in the groin and tumbling you in an indignified heap to the floor.

Curiously enough this action is also followed by the word 'Ohphookimle'. The less lucky among you will find that you successfully career the length of the room at an angle of 45 degrees, only to come to rest when you smash against the cooker and fall to the floor. A popular addition to this movement is to catch the frying pan handle under your armpit as you fall and catapult it across the room.

At this point a spasmodic knocking will be heard from either the floor or the ceiling. This is only the neighbours and should be ignored.

Do not play music unless you have a tape deck!

It is inevitable that you will want to listen to your absolutely favourite record and it can be distressing to hear it go 'Zeeeet!' It doesn't matter what the record is, or how carefully you lower the needle, the end result is always 'Zeeeet!' Even more distressing than this is when you quickly remove the needle and hear your favourite record go 'Ferdump! Dump! Zeeeet!' The end result of all this is a loud exclamation of 'Ohphookimle'. The record is then picked up with as many fingers on the recording area as possible and placed, sleeveless, on the floor.

As you straighten up you will suddenly realize that all the exciting activity has made you feel rather queasy. You should make your way to the sink as quickly as possible.

Removal of the pots from the sink is recommended and the usual position is to stand with the legs apart and the knees locked as you hold on to both taps. Most people at this point turn very spiritual and cry out to God. 'Oh God!' Be assured that you will not be answered. How would you like it if your friends only got in touch with you when they were heaving in the sink? 'Oh Daaave!' 'Oh Fraaank!' No miracles can be expected at this point.

Some people now find themselves with an urge to douse their face with cold water. This doesn't do a great deal of good, but rubbing your cold hands on your face and making a noise like 'Flubbery flubbery' can be very satisfying.

It is now time to go to bed.

DO NOT STAND UP!

As stated before, the best way to cross the room is on all fours. Those people who have not followed this advice will find themselves on the bed. That sickening thud was when their head hit the wall. The more wise amongst you will have managed to assume Position 6.

Now remove your clothes.

DO NOT STAND UP!

If you stand up while trying to remove your jeans you will only end up head butting the cooker again. Only this time you will have hopped at high speed across the room.

If you can remove your clothes successfully then good luck. If you can't, don't worry. Just leave the light on, leave the record player going 'Hummmm', leave the tap running and leave all your clothes on.

How else will you know just what a great time you had last night?

CHAPTER NINE

BEING 'NOT DRUNK'

Being 'not drunk' requires a great deal of effort and is usually found among people who live in shared houses. Being 'not drunk' requires the person that is suffering from abuse of alcohol to impress on his fellow inhabitants that they are in fact quite sober, when what they would really like to do is fall down.

The usual course of action is to enter the building as quietly as possible. This can be done if a great deal of concentration is brought to bear on getting the key in the lock. Once inside the doorway a deep breath should be taken in order to brace yourself before walking into the communal living-room.

If you were actually sober you would normally walk into the living-room and nod a slight greeting before walking through to the kitchen. However, because you are being 'not drunk' you should walk into the living-room and place your hands firmly across the back of the settee, saying, 'All right. Anything interesting been on?' as you try and focus on the television. (Being conversational in a shared house at night is a sure sign of being 'not drunk'.)

Having convinced yourself that you have convinced everyone else how sober you are you should then hover for a further 30 seconds, staring at the television as if it was the most interesting thing you had seen for ages. It is usually at this point that you realize you are watching *Come Dancing*. If this is so then you can be sure that the people watching the television are being 'not drunk' too.

You should then have a desire to make a cup of coffee, or in fact anything to get you out of the room. You should suddenly stand upright and say 'Well. I think I'll have a coffee'.

. . . .

Never, ever, does anyone say 'Well. I think I'll have a coffee' unless they are being 'not drunk'. They'd normally just go and get one.

. . . .

Having dismissed yourself from the room you can then go through to the kitchen. Try not to breathe too heavily with relief as you will require all your faculties in the kitchen.

Being 'not drunk' in the kitchen is very dangerous and should be done with great care.

The most popular starting position for being 'not drunk' in the kitchen is to either stand in the middle of the floor, or stand immediately in front of the sink. A completely blank expression should then be allowed to form on your face and a very slow rocking motion should start at the ankles. The rocking motion should be almost imperceptible and allowed to build up gradually until you are swaying back and forth like an inflatable dummy with sand in its base.

At the point where you have to put one foot behind you to stop yourself falling over you should exclaim, 'Coffee!' and walk once round the kitchen for no reason whatsoever. When you find yourself at the sink again the most common action is to open every kitchen unit door, saying, 'Coffee coffee coffee', as you do so. You will then realize you are slamming doors shut and quickly stop doing so, also lowering your voice to a whispered 'Coffee coffee coffee'.

There is a strong urge to fill the kettle at this point. Even though the coffee hasn't yet been found. It is probably a good idea to fill it while you think of it. It is also a popular move to fill the kettle with enough water for eight cups of coffee. This will give you plenty of time to wait angrily for it to boil.

The kettle business now having been set in motion, preferably after forgetting to plug it in or light the gas, you should now begin to look for a cup. It should be noted that never, at any time, while being 'not drunk' in the kitchen will you ever be able to find a clean mug. It is against the

60

laws of nature
and shouldn't be allowed to worry you.

Simply pick up the nearest mug you find,
dismiss from your mind who it belongs to and
sniff the remnants of the cold murky liquid still
in it. The sniff is done, not so much to enlighten
you as to what the liquid is, but because it is
impossible to pick up a mug when being 'not
drunk' without actually sniffing it.

You should then pour the liquid distastefully
down the gap between all the mucky plates and
the sink and turn on the tap hard enough for a
spray of water to shoot up off a teaspoon and soak
you.

Now is a good time to light the kettle although this can be left until you've stood around a little longer wondering why it hasn't boiled.

By now the coffee should have miraculously appeared in front of your face on the formica work surface. The fact that it doesn't belong to you should only be taken into account if being 'not drunk' when others are in the kitchen. Especially if the other people present own the coffee.

Also, if you are not in the presence of anyone else it is quite acceptable for half the spoon of coffee to go in the mug and half to go all over the work surface. Simply sweep the surplus on to the floor. No one will notice as all shared kitchens have crunchy floors anyway.

Now is also a good time to light the kettle, although by now you should be becoming irritable and not really want a coffee anyway. Simply leave the kettle on and stroll out of the kitchen. The tap should be left running.

If you have to pass through the communal living-room be sure to say something inane which nobody is listening to like, 'Well. I'm off to bed now.'

Having negotiated the stairs successfully, see 'How To Be Drunk in a Bedsit'.

CHAPTER TEN

SPRING CLEANING

Spring cleaning is what people in real houses do in April. Spring Cleaning in a bedsit is what people do in July or any other time when the temperature reaches a heady 60 degrees Fahrenheit. This is an arduous task and can take you the best part of an hour.

The first thing to do is take down your plastic bag double glazing so that you can actually see what you are doing. The plastic bags, having been left up all winter, will be coated with grease and cigarette smoke, halving the light that came through the window in the first place. Because this brown film builds up slowly you will not notice it yourself until friends come round and start bumping into the furniture.

The next thing to do is to take out all the strips of newspaper that you jammed into the window frame last Christmas. These, you may remember, were put there to stop the draught blowing your paper lampshade around and making you feel seasick. When you have wasted half an hour reading the news headlines from last Christmas you should then proceed to try and open the window.

Clamp your jaw firmly and bash the heel of your hand against the outside of the frame. Care should be taken when doing this as blood is quite difficult to get off carpets. Now undo all the catches on the window and try again.

By this time you should have remembered that this is the window that doesn't open anyway. Repeat the whole process again until you either open the next window along, or put your fist through it. Either way, the result is that a clear substance rushes into the room. This is 'air' and shouldn't be allowed to worry you unduly. The part of the air that is pleasant to breathe and doesn't smell of old socks and fried food is called 'oxygen'. This is jolly good stuff and should be breathed slowly as you won't be used to it. Oxygen tends to make you think of *The Sound Of Music*. Don't be alarmed. This will wear off.

The next stage of

Spring Cleaning is to find the vacuum cleaner. The best way to find the vacuum cleaner is to pretend you aren't looking for it. It will then miraculously appear. If you decide beforehand, 'Right. I will look for the vacuum cleaner', you may as well give up because you haven't got a chance.

Having found the vacuum cleaner, you can go about the task of clearing up all the cobwebs you never noticed because it was too dark. It can be quite heart-rending knowing you are making some poor little spider homeless (how would you like it if you came back from the shops to find someone had vacuumed up your bedsit?), but it has to be done so that you can find the LP you lost six months ago.

Once you have had a good vacuum round and bashed the skirting board enough to annoy everyone in the house you should put the vacuum cleaner back where you found it. In the bath, on the stairs, or in the middle of the corridor. This will ensure that if anyone is looking for the vacuum cleaner, they won't be able to find it either.

Now comes the problem of finding storage space for your three duffel coats, five pullovers and twenty pairs of mountaineering socks, as they won't be needed until autumn ie August. If you stand on a chair you should be able to ram them between the suitcase on the wardrobe and the ceiling.

If it isn't possible to get them on the wardrobe because of all the supermarket boxes you should place them on the floor somewhere and when you have walked round them for a few weeks you'll hardly notice they are there. In fact, by autumn you'll have forgotten where you put them and will be looking all over the place.

Now is a good time to make a cup of tea and sit quietly in a chair. It can be quite a shock after spring cleaning to find you can now do all sorts of things you couldn't do before. Like being able to see and breathe.

THE BEDSIT VACUUM CLEANER

T he bedsit vacuum cleaner is a scientific phenomenon in its own right and usually resides in a forbidding black hole under the stairs. Unless you are looking for it.

The bedsit vacuum cleaner has the uncanny ability to disappear and materialize in different places in the house. No matter where you saw it five minutes ago it will not be there when you go to get it. This leads to the distasteful task of knocking on everyone's door and asking if anyone has seen it. Everyone will look at you blankly and mumble something about it 'usually' being under the stairs. When you finally give up and go back to check the hole under the stairs, it will be sitting in the middle of the corridor as if it had been there all the time.

Do not be alarmed by the huge sausage thing on the back of it. This is the dust bag and will require emptying. It will always require emptying. Always. Without fail. Every bloody time.

Simply spend 20 minutes pressing likely buttons and levers trying to get the lid off and then go 'Oh' as it all suddenly collapses and flops a pile of dust on to the carpet. Then take the bag thing and transport it at arm's length to the dustbin. Which will also need emptying.

One of the great mysteries of life will become evident to you as you empty the pile of dust and bits into the bin. That is: Where do all the pubic hairs come from?

Cavemen must have been knee-deep in the things and they didn't know where they came from either. (Have you ever wondered what coconut mats were made from?) Don't worry about it too much. Nobody knows where they all come from.

(What *are* coconut mats made from?)

· ·

The 'rickety tickety rickety' sound is a pebble that is built into the vacuum cleaner and goes round and round to give you the impression that you are actually picking things up with it.

Anyway, now comes the time to try and put the bag back in the vacuum cleaner. Having already seen how the bag comes off this should be relatively easy and only take 25 minutes or so. When the dust bag is refitted you can go about the task of vacuuming the room. This usually involves a frenzy of activity as you kick things out of the way trying the find the floor.

It can be a great deal of fun seeing how hard you can hit the furniture with the vacuum cleaner and also seeing how loud you can get it to sound when you bang the skirting board. You will notice the person upstairs doing this all the time. Especially when you are listening to a quiet piece of music or trying to think.

THE CARPET SWEEPER

T his strange thing has similar properties to the vacuum cleaner in that you can never find it when you are looking for it. Should you actually find it, what you then do is push it backwards and forwards across the room trying to pick things up. Anything.

After a short period the carpet sweeper will deposit a long sausage of pubic hair and crumbs on your carpet. Carpet sweepers don't actually seem to pick anything up so it is assumed that dumping long sausages of crumbs and pubic hair on your carpet is what they are really for. (Their only real use is for bashing against the skirting board to annoy the people downstairs.)

CHAPTER ELEVEN

LETTERS

W hen you first move into a bedsit you will not receive any letters for the first few weeks. Then, in spite of the fact that the DHSS don't know where you are, your mother doesn't know where you are and your best friend doesn't know where you are, you will receive a letter telling you that 'you and only you' have been chosen to possess a Lucky Draw Number which will be drawn out of a barrel if you send back the pre-addressed envelope with a 'YES' sticker attached. It is very flattering to think that the CIA and MI5 have passed on your address to a catalogue company.

Although you will not receive a great deal of mail yourself you will notice every morning that most of the letters that do arrive at the house are brown with a see-through window. People in bedsits only have friends that write to them using brown envelopes with see-through windows.

The most common friend that people in bedsits have is a man who signs himself on the front of the envelope as TV LICENCE. The other one is a man with the initials DHSS.

One of the fascinating things about letters arriving at bedsits is that although you have lived there for ages you have never heard of half the people that the letters are for. Even more curious is that the letters disappear.

The most common writer of letters to people that don't exist is Mr TV LICENCE, who must be very lonely because sometimes he doesn't even care who writes back and addresses the

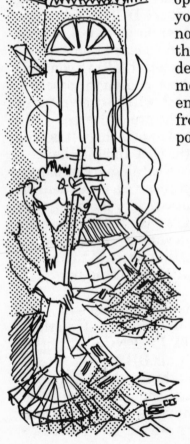

letter with a cry for help to The Occupier. If you open one of these letters you will realize why nobody writes back to the poor man. He keeps demanding money with menaces. The only enjoyment to be gained from these letters is to post them again and see how long it takes them to come back.

Bedsitland is one of the few places where you can find out where people 'used' to live without asking them. Their letters always have scribbled out addresses on them. This is useful for getting in touch with people's ex-wives and other jokes like that.

CHAPTER TWELVE

THE TIMER SWITCH

The Timer Switch is a device installed on the stairs. When you press the button it will turn the light on just long enough for you to get halfway up the stairs and be plunged into total darkness. If you then feel for the wall or fumble for the stairs you will be able to make your way to the first landing.

Somewhere around the landing is another timer switch. It is usually placed exactly where you don't expect it and can take some minutes to find. It is also quite common, as you grope along the wall, to find that a door opens in front of your face, leaving you mumbling to the startled person coming out of the room that you were 'just looking for the light'. This encounter is especially effective if you are calling on a friend on your way to a fancy dress party and happen to be dressed as a gorilla.

Should nobody come to the door to find out what the funny noise is, you will have to find the landing timer switch. A good way to do this is to fumble round striking matches while calling your landlord a tight-fisted git for having a timer switch.

When you do find the landing timer switch

the stairs will suddenly light up just long enough for you to not quite reach your room. At this point you should resort to fumbling all over the door with the tip of your Yale key trying to find the key hole that you distinctly felt with the tip of your left forefinger.

If you are drunk and coming back to a bedsit that has timer switches it is best to start off on all fours at the bottom of the stairs and crawl up in complete darkness by memory, until you stop in front of where you think your door is, or head butt a drunk coming the other way.

Timer switches are particularly hazardous when going out at night. The usual thing to do is to look round the room, check your pockets, check you have your keys and then,

72

after turning off the light, walk briskly out on to the landing, shutting the door behind you. You will then think you have gone blind.

No matter which room you live in the landing timer switch will not be outside your room. It will be along the landing and result in your having to gingerly finger your way along the wall in complete darkness until you find it. (It can be fun not telling your friends about this and listening to them falling down the stairs.) However, having pressed the timer switch on your way out the stairs will be illuminated just long enough for you to fall down the last three steps.

A good way of combating the effect of a Timer Switch is to jam it with matches. This has a dual effect. It keeps the light on all night so that you can see the stairs and it makes the landlord very very mad. Both of which are good things.

Another good way of combating the effect of a Timer Switch is to rip it off the wall and hurl it down the stairs. This will leave the stairs in total darkness but you'll hardly notice the difference.

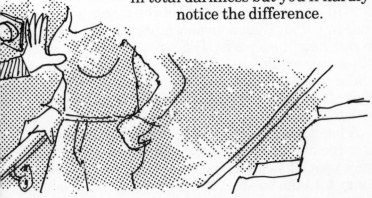

CHAPTER THIRTEEN

THE METER

The meter is a grey box in the corner of the room that hates you. It will need to be fed with money at every opportunity and if you fail to do this it will either plunge you into darkness or cut off your supply of heat. If the heat is cut off in a bedsit it can result in death. There is no way round this problem unless you want to end up in prison, where your heating and lighting are paid for anyway.

If the landlord comes round to empty the meter while you are there, be sure to avert your eyes when the money box is opened. This will prevent you seeing the landlord in a strange orgasmic state and also save you from crying when you see the hundreds of pounds you have put into the thing.

All meters are battleship grey. This is so that you will have no illusions about the meter being anything other than a vicious money-grabbing tin can, hogging a perfectly good space where your stereo would have fitted. Some meters do lurk in cupboards but this is to give you a false sense of security and make it harder to find when the lights go off.

A lot of meters are built so that you have to place the money in the slot and then turn a small lever, which blocks off the hole and thrusts your money into the box, never to be seen again. You

can be sure that the lever is always in the wrong
position and yet you will still try and press the
coin into the slot at least twice before turning the
lever to the correct position. This happens every
single time, even when you think you know
which way the lever should be before putting
your money in.

A lot of people spend a great deal of time
thinking of ways to get into the meter. This

. . . .

*The ON/OFF switch for
the fuse box is
sometimes near the
meter. When you are
bored you can put a
record on and switch it
up and down to make
your record player go
'Woooeeer Woooeeer'.
This is especially
effective with Human
League singles.*

should only be done with any sincerity if you are planning on leaving the country for a long time. Preferably to Brazil. However, it should be noted that the slot meter is made of the same stuff that is used to make armour piercing shells and such puny devices as sledgehammers and crowbars should be forgotten.

The only really effective way to get into a slot meter is to place the 'chair' in the middle of the floor and hide behind it while you obliterate the meter with high explosives. If you do this while the Heavy Metal Hero is playing his music nobody will hear it.

Games to play with meters

1. See if you can put money in quick enough to keep an electric fire going.

2. Set up a stroboscope to make it look as if the fly wheel is going slower.

3. Paint the meter red or yellow and see how long it takes the landlord to find it.

4. Watch the units hand and pretend it is an altimeter on a plane that is crashing.

CHAPTER FOURTEEN

HABITS

P eople who have lived in bedsits for a time are recognizable by their habits. You can't take them anywhere.

THE SNIFF

T his has nothing to do with sitting miserably in front of the fire fighting off a cold. The Sniff is caused by never knowing if the milk you are going to put in your tea is fresh or not. After several years of picking up milk cartons and sniffing to see if they are fresh, it becomes impossible to do otherwise. Even when you have just bought the milk from a dairy.

The Sniff can be embarrassing when you go round to see posh relatives. They take particular offence to you sniffing the milk jug before pouring milk into your tea.

Another big problem of the Sniff is that it spreads to other areas until you find yourself sniffing just about anything you pick up. Especially cold cups of coffee, just before you throw them away, even when you know it is just a cold cup of coffee.

Really big problems start when you begin sniffing the radio and gas fire to see if they are fresh.

THE BREATH TEST

T his has nothing to do with halitosis. This is
the habit of sticking your head out of the
duvet and breathing out to see if vapour forms.
This is to give you an indication of how many
pairs of socks you can take off before getting out
of bed.

The Breath Test is particularly good for
convincing yourself that it is far too cold to get
out of bed and that you didn't really want to go to
work anyway.

THE OVER DRESS

T he Over Dress is quite common amongst
people who live in bedsits and tends to
happen in summer.

. . . .

*'Summer' is those four
days in July when you
can't see the breath
coming out of your mouth.
(See The Breath Test.)*

. . . .

The Over Dress is the habit of wearing more
clothes than you need to when you go out, due to
the fact that the temperature in your bedsit is 20

78

degrees colder than the rest of the world. It is very embarrassing to find yourself wearing a coat and pullover when everyone else is wearing T-shirt and shorts. (Explaining this away by saying you have just come back from Canada only works for a short time.)

THE DOOR LOCK

T his is the habit of trying to lock the door behind you no matter what room you go into. Friends find it particularly intriguing when you reach for a non-existent key to lock yourself into their living room. They don't understand that you normally have two sets of doors to lock and unlock. If they did they wouldn't leave the door to your 'home' wide open when they came to visit.

THE BUGGER OFF

T his is the embarrassing habit caused by living in bedsits surrounded by drunks and neighbours like the Nuisance. It is the habit of turning over in your sleep at the slightest noise and shouting 'Bugger Off!'

This has caused many people to wake up single in the morning when they were sure they went to bed with somebody.

CHAPTER FIFTEEN

SICKNESS

When you become sick in a bedsit you become *sick*! This isn't sick as in drinking too much. This is sick as in feeling horrible. The reason you become so sick is because you are on your own and there is nobody to tell you just how overdramatic you are being, leaving you to feel sorry for yourself with Oscar-winning abandon. The most common illness is Flu. This is not the 'flu' that lasts a day and comes on when you don't want to go to work.

This is Flu!

Flu is short for influenza and is caused by little things coming down your chimney and going up your nose. As in, 'Up your flu'. (All right. It isn't.) Flu is: A catarrhal inflammation of the mucous membranes of the air passage, attended by fever and nervous prostration. Which is the same thing really.

If you feel the first signs of flu you should immediately go to the shops and buy the following:

Flu Survival Kit

1 bottle of aspirin.   Food for four days.

Lots of lemon things.   1 bottle of Benylin.

Radio batteries.   1 good book.   ½ bottle of whisky.

80

The food is so that you don't have to leave the house until it's all over. The good book and radio batteries are to give you something to do. The aspirin is to break the fever. The lemon things are so that you can say 'Yes' when everybody asks you afterwards if you took any lemon things and the Benylin is for getting smashed on when the whisky runs out.

. . . .

The first sign of Flu is when all of a sudden you feel cold and think a mouse has run up and down inside your shirt.

. . . .

When the full symptoms of Flu take control you should retire to bed immediately. Surround yourself with the Flu Survival Kit and brace yourself for the first fever attack. As you lie there sweating, try and remember every detail of how it feels. It may be the last time you experience warmth for a long time, especially in winter.

When the fever attack subsides, wrap the duvet around yourself and go to the cooker to put the kettle on. You should then slump in the chair with the duvet still around you and sniff miserably so that you know just how ill you are. From the chair you can then stagger dejectedly

81

back to the kettle and either make a drink of tea with lots of whisky in it, or a lemon thing. Be sure to catch sight of your poor forlorn face in the mirror as you shuffle back to bed. Say something pathetic like 'Nobody cares if I die' and curl up in the duvet after putting the radio on.

If you decide to listen to the radio *do not* tune to a commercial station. The lemon thing will have made you drowsy and you can guarantee that every time you drift out of your semi-conscious stupor there will be a Beecham's Powders advert blaring in your ear. 'Do you feel feverish? Shivery? Does your body ache?' 'Yes! Bugger off!'

It should then suddenly occur to you that you haven't rung work to tell them you have Flu. Do not worry. Always leave this until the second day because (a) You will feel better and be able to face going to the telephone. (b) Nobody will believe you anyway.

The unfortunate thing about ringing work to tell them you are ill is that you have to actually leave the house to do it. If you are genuinely feeling terrible this is the last thing you feel like doing, next to going swimming. Not only that, but the middle management jerk that you are trying to convince can't understand why you didn't phone the day before because he (a) has a phone of his own; (b) has a spouse to lie for him; (c) is a workaholic and would have to be dead to take a day off work anyway.

Don't let this bother you. Have another lemon thing and go back to bed.

By the second day you will be feeling slightly better and realize you haven't eaten anything for 48 hours. This is because you are living on your own and haven't got someone trying to force soup and other nourishing things down you every five minutes. (It's also about now you start missing your mother.) Do not cook anything big as you will have changed your mind by the time you come to eat it.

The best thing to have is soup and bread. This will allow you to feel really sorry for yourself.

Having eaten something, you will start to feel more alert, more active, and bored to death. This is where the good book comes in handy.

Something earthy yet controversial that inspires and leaves you wanting more is recommended. Like *The Diary of Adrian Mole*.

As you curl up in bed again it should suddenly occur to you that not one person has knocked on your door. Not one single person has been round for two days. No friends have called unexpectedly during your favourite programme. The Nuisance hasn't asked you for a cup of sugar and your best friend has gone on holiday for two weeks.

You could have been dead!!

You realize that your poor mutilated body could have slumped to the floor with a mad axeman's axe sticking out of your back and not one single person would know about it! Panic starts setting in and you begin to think of all sorts of ways to inform the outside world of your condition just in case you were really dying.

A really good way is to run up and down the street shouting 'I'm dying!' but nobody will believe you. Another good method is to fasten a message to a brick and throw it through your window. (This doesn't work if you face on to the back alley of an Indian restaurant.) The message should be short and yet profound, portraying your desperate condition with a mixture of irony and pathos. Something like 'I'm dying!' will do. If that fails, try flashing your light on and off to signal SOS. This will work, but only if your room faces somebody that used to be in the Merchant Navy and your light bulb holds out.

Having decided that it is possible to get help if you really need it, you can then relax and get back to having Flu.

By the third day you will be feeling a lot better and be able to go to the pub for a medicinal drink and a packet of crisps. It should also occur to you that you just might be able to stretch your illness to four days. This involves complications like doctor's notes and should only be considered if either your doctor or your boss is an idiot.

By the fourth day you will have almost fully recovered, other than the headache from drinking the bottle of Benylin and the rest of the whisky. Around about this time you should also notice that all your friends turn up, the Nuisance knocks on your door and several people you have never seen before come round just when you don't need them. Put it down to one of those things and hope they catch Flu.

HURT HAND

When you live on your own and hurt your best hand, life becomes very difficult. However, with all those hours off work you will be able to think up many varied and exciting ways of killing the person who invented the childproof aspirin bottle.

It won't occur to you until you only have one hand available that getting dressed and undressed is very difficult. It is also very difficult to play the violin, which is no great loss anyway and if you never did play the violin now is not the time to start. Even more difficult than playing the violin is fastening your shoes. Fastening your shoelaces with one hand is very much like playing the violin only you don't get the horrible noises. The horrible noises that you do get will be coming from you as you try to hold one lace in your teeth and fasten a knot with your good hand.

A way of overcoming this is to wear elasticated shoes or slippers.

How to open a childproof aspirin bottle

1. Take the bottle and place it under your armpit.

2. Use your good hand to turn the top until it goes 'Clickety clickety'.

3. Press harder on the top until the bottle shoots out from under your armpit and disappears across the room.

4. Retrieve the bottle and kneel on the floor with it jammed between your knees.

5. Use your good hand to turn the top until it goes 'Clickety clickety'.

6. Press even harder on the top until the bottle flips over and stubs your thumb on the floor.

7. Swear loudly.

8. Hold the bottle in your good hand and try turning the top with your teeth until it goes 'Clickety clickety'.

9. Allow the bottle to slip slightly so that it makes a horrible sound on your teeth and crashes into your gums.

10. Throw the bottle very hard against the fireplace until it smashes.

11. Take as many aspirins as you require.

   (*Note:* Fireplaces should be kept out of reach of children.)

Another big problem is trying to button a shirt. This is nothing like playing the violin but is very difficult nevertheless. A way of overcoming the difficulty of fastening buttons on a shirt is to sellotape the front of the shirt shut. This is very effective if you can get the sellotape off the reel with one hand, but it looks very silly. A better way of overcoming the problem is to wear the black bri-nylon polo neck pullover that your aunt bought last Christmas and you haven't worn since.

If your arm is in a sling, wearing the black polo neck will make it look as if you have lost an arm. This is no bad thing as it will deter old ladies from pushing in front of you at the bus stop by shuffling slowly up the outside of the queue and pretending they didn't realize they were doing it.

If you normally wear tight jeans you will find it impossible to put them on. This usually means that you have to wear the baggy black ones that you wouldn't be seen dead in.

Such a combination of clothes will look ridiculous. It is therefore suggested that if you need to go to the shops you should wear dark glasses, so that nobody will think you are a violinist. (**Note:** Dark glasses, black polo neck, black trousers and slip on shoes are the dress of the Beatnik. The Beatnik fashion was actually started by a man in a bedsit that had hurt his hand. Beatniks do not play the violin.)

HURT FOOT

T he only really bad thing about having a Hurt
Foot is that you can still play the violin. This
is not recommended. It is very unnatural to play
the violin with your feet and you won't be able to
run away when people start hammering your
door down.

The advantage of having a plaster cast on
your leg is that you only get Bedsit Shin on one
shin bone. However, with an open-toed plaster
cast you are likely to get Bedsit Toe or frost bite.

• •

*Kung Fu should not be
practised with a plaster
cast on your foot. The
momentum will rip your
leg off.*

• •

If any friends come round to see how you are,
try not to get angry when every single one of
them insists on having a go on your crutch and
then holds it up pretending it is a machine gun.
This is quite common and you would only do the
same if someone else had a broken foot. Also,
after hearing 'Aaargh Jim lad' more than 20
times, try not to hit anyone with your good hand.

Interesting things to do with your crutch

1. Pretend you are a Dalek.

2. Point it at the lady across the road at night.

3. Bang on the ceiling with it, just underneath the record player, and see if you can get the record to jump.

4. Put a shoe on it and make footprints on the ceiling in the hall.

5. Lean out of the window and tap on the window of the next bedsit along. This is especially effective if you live on the third floor.

6. Avoid Bedsit Hand by sticking a match to the end of it and lighting the gas fire with that instead.

7. Paint it white and see how many crashes you can cause when you leap out into the middle of the road waving it.

If you must hit anyone, hit them with your crutch.

After a while you will become quite attached to your crutch. You will find that you can play with it for hours, doing such things as turning the television on and off with it. Your crutch will become part of you and you'll wonder how you ever managed without one.

89

CHAPTER SIXTEEN

SEX IN A BEDSIT

Indulging in sex in a bedsit is like trying to arrange flowers while parachuting. There are so many reasons why it will be a disaster that very often it is easier to claim you are a monk and forget the whole thing.

The bedsit bed is the biggest culprit in destroying a wonderful evening. Just lying on the bed is dangerous enough, so the risks involved in jigging up and down on the thing are tenfold.

Several different injuries can result from indulging in sex on a bedsit bed.

BANANA BACK

This is caused by trying to make love on a Flop Drop mattress. Because of the slump in the middle of the mattress your feet and head end up a foot higher than your pelvis, resulting in a dramatic curving of the spine and an excruciating pain in the back.

People suffering from Banana Back are easily identifiable by the way they walk around constantly looking at the ceiling, or the floor, depending on their position preference.

HEADBOARD FINGER

T his is caused when you try to stop the headboard cracking rhythmically against the wall as you tell your partner how much you love them with words like 'Oomph'. It is just at the point when you least need it that you realize the headboard is making a noise like a pile driver. Instinctively you will reach out to stop it. Unfortunately it won't occur to you until the next 'Oomph' that there is the momentum of two bodies and a bed smashing your fingers into the wall.

The most common reaction to this is to wave your hand in the air and swear inventively. This is particularly useful if your lover likes you to talk dirty.

A similar complaint is Tailboard Foot. This is caused by trying to stop the headboard banging by applying pressure to the tailboard with your foot. This results in a form of cramp, where your toes and heel try to meet in the middle of your foot. The pain of this cramp in your foot makes you exhale in agony and grab hold of the headboard. The headboard then smashes your fingers into the wall.

Should you still be able to go through the motions of making love in spite of going into spasms of pain your lover will think they are doing a great job. After all, it's not everyone that they can get to moan in ecstasy and writhe around all over the bed.

SQUEAK SPINE

T his is a sinister condition that gives you back
ache for weeks without knowing why. Your
partner will think you are the slowest, sleaziest,
most considerate, most sensitive lover they have
ever had, whereas what you are really doing is
trying to stop the bed from squeaking.

This predicament results in a posture that
looks as if you were trying to hold the bed to the
floor with your feet and hands while trying to stir
porridge with your pelvis. Don't worry if you
start crying from the pain. Your lover will think
you are in romantic bliss.

A lot of people try and overcome the Squeak
by oiling the joints of the bed. This is not
recommended as all it does is allow the bed to
slowly walk along the floor until it is banging
against the door. This can be particularly
embarrassing if your door opens outwards.

HOT KNEE

T his painful condition is caused by using
nylon sheets on a Rock mattress. It can also
occur from giving up on the bed and trying out
the floor. It is a condition that occurs when the
knee bone rubs on the nylon surface and nearly
sets on fire from the heat. This condition is
dangerous because it is easy to ignore while
engaged in erotic activity. However, an hour
later you will be unable to walk without looking
like both your legs are in splints.

If your lover is in the nude and a Jehovah's witness comes round, invite them in. The world record for keeping a straight face is 23 seconds.

SINGLE BED TWINGE

T his condition occurs mostly in single beds. This is caused when your partner turns over in their sleep and knees you in the groin. The result of this is for both your knees to come up smartly to your stomach and smack them under the chin. This is handy if you wish to terminate the relationship.

BEDSIT BIT FINGER

T his condition is very painful and is the result of being bitten on the hand. The reason for being bitten on the hand is from placing it flat over your partner's mouth to stop them screaming out.

It is very flattering to think that you are the cause of their wild screams but it is usually because they've got their hair caught in the springs, or the headboard keeps smacking them on the back of the head when it comes back off the wall.

A PUNCH IN THE NOSE

T his is caused by making love to the Heavy Metal Hero's girlfriend.

NEIGHBOURS INDULGING

A lot of fun can be had when other people in the house are indulging in late-night sex. One of the best laughs is to tape record their

94

groans through the wall and play it back to them at full volume when they have finished.

Another good joke is to wait until they nearly reach the point of no return and then let out a blood-curdling scream as if you are being murdered. Be sure not to laugh when the bed suddenly stops squeaking.

An alternative to the scream is to go out on the landing and shout 'I know she's here somewhere. I'll kill her!'

If the neighbours are particularly raucous and the female is particularly loud, a whole evening's entertainment can be had from phoning the police and telling them that you think someone next door is being murdered. Be sure to do this early in the proceedings so the police will have a chance to actually hear her being murdered and sledgehammer the door in.

It is also worthwhile looking for an LP of live music with lots of applause and 'More! More!' and then playing it at full blast when they have finished.

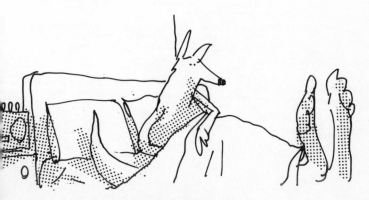

And Finally

Things to remember:

1. Don't cook cabbage.

2. Don't play violin.

3. Don't bet on horses that lose.

4. If you find a peanut with lots of legs don't eat it.

5. Landlords have to be foreign for tax reasons.

6. You are not kidding anyone. Cannabis plants do not look anything like tomato plants.